FIBONACCI DESIGNS·1
COLORING·BOOK

I0786334

ARTIST · INFO

ISBN-13: 978-1717395269
COPYRIGHT © 2018

ALL PAGES ARE CENTERED
BETWEEN EDGE AND DOTTED LINE
CUT ALONG DOTTED LINE TO REMOVE

THIS IS YOUR TEST PAGE

TRY-OUT PENCILS, PENS, MARKERS, PAINTS, ETC.

PLACE BLANK PAPER BETWEEN PAGES TO PREVENT BLEED-THROUGH

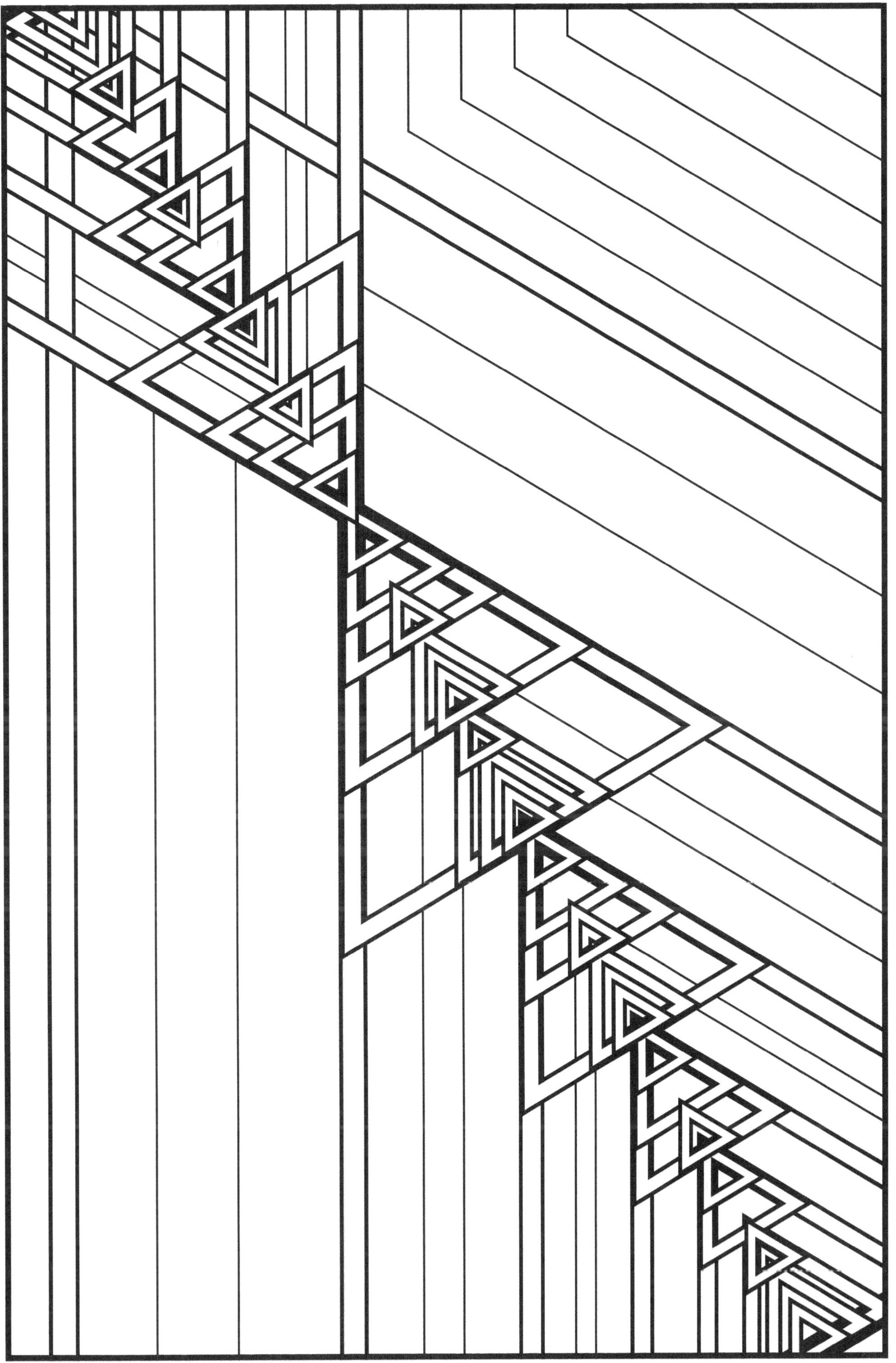

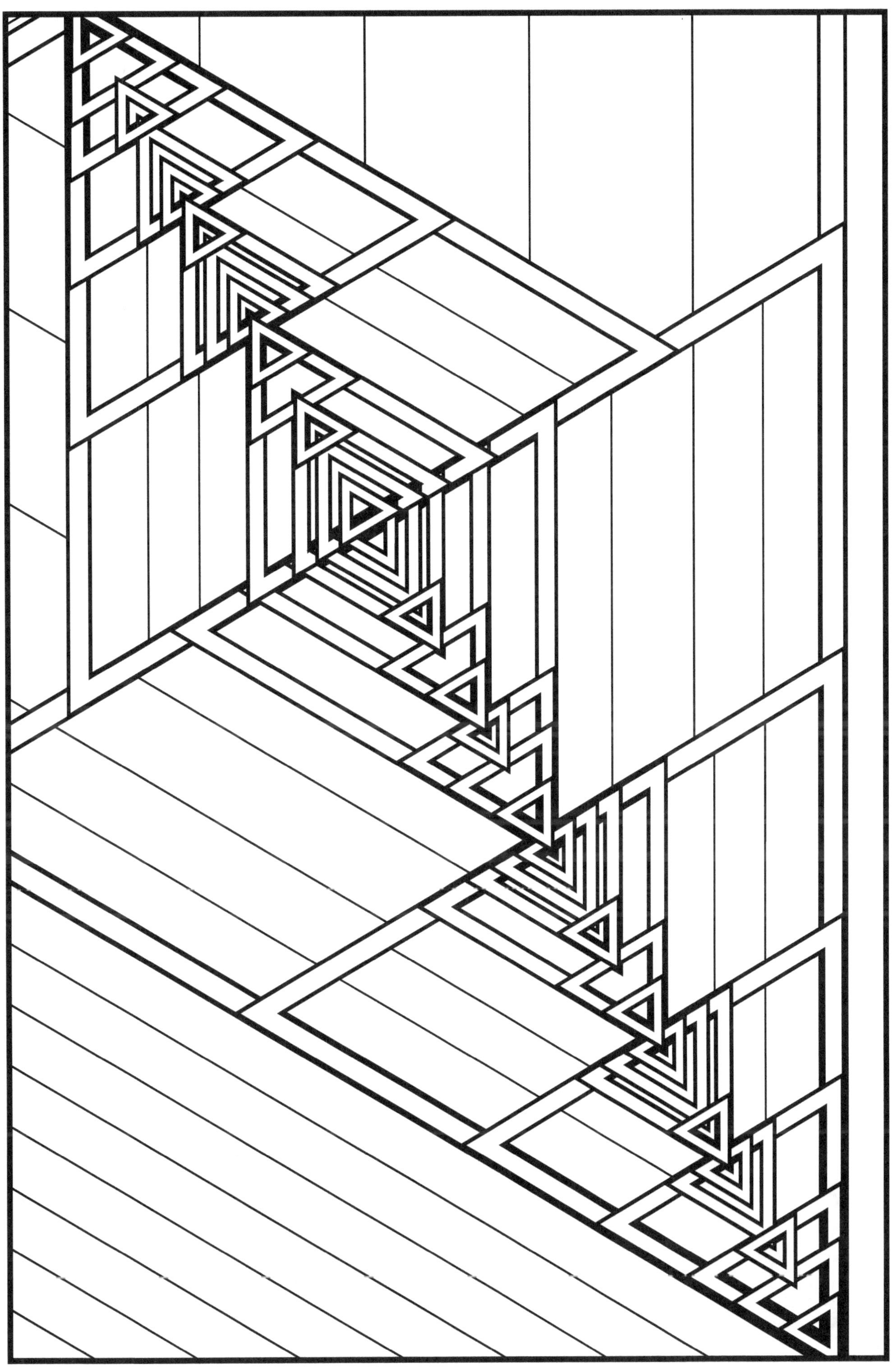

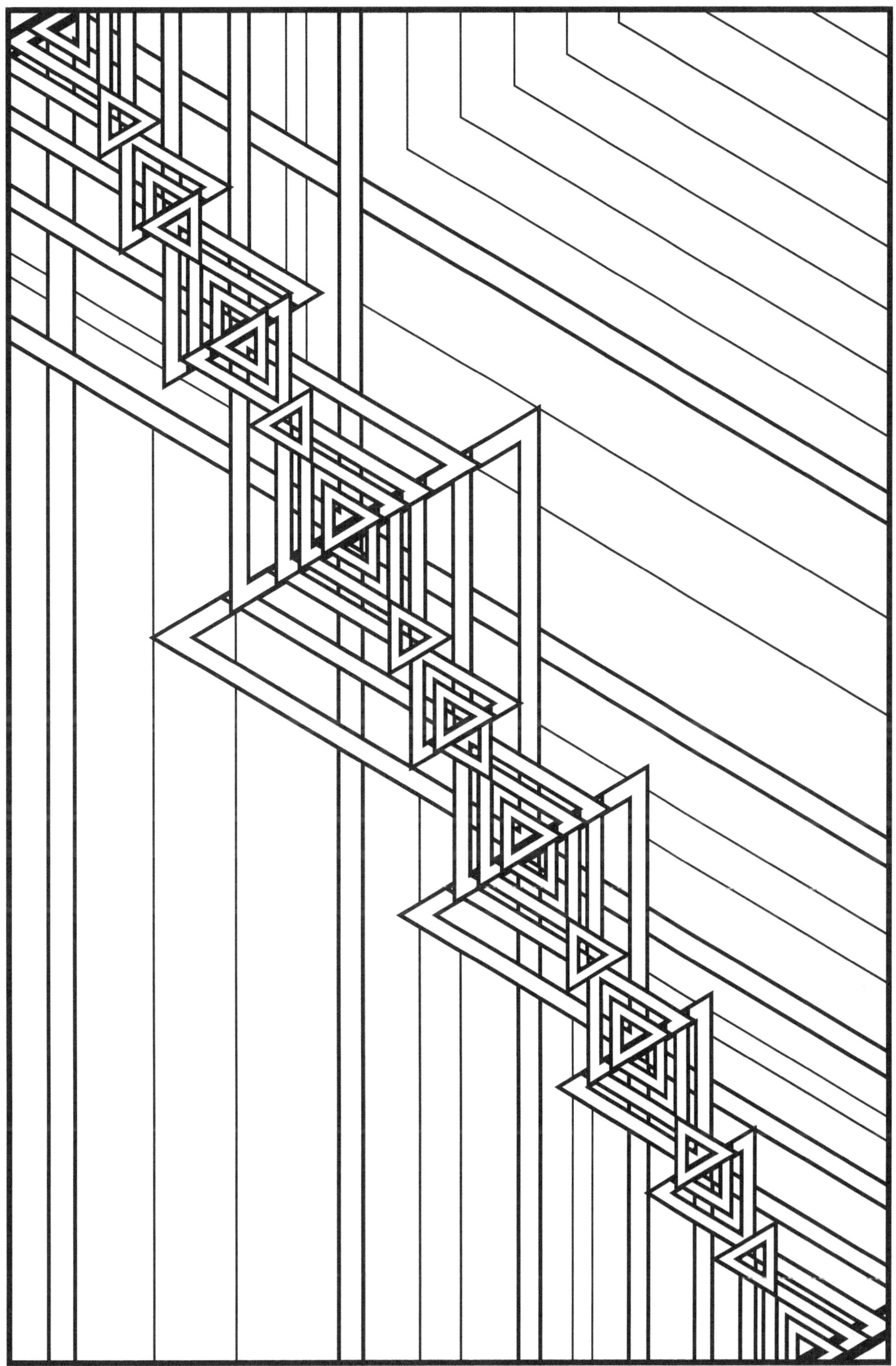

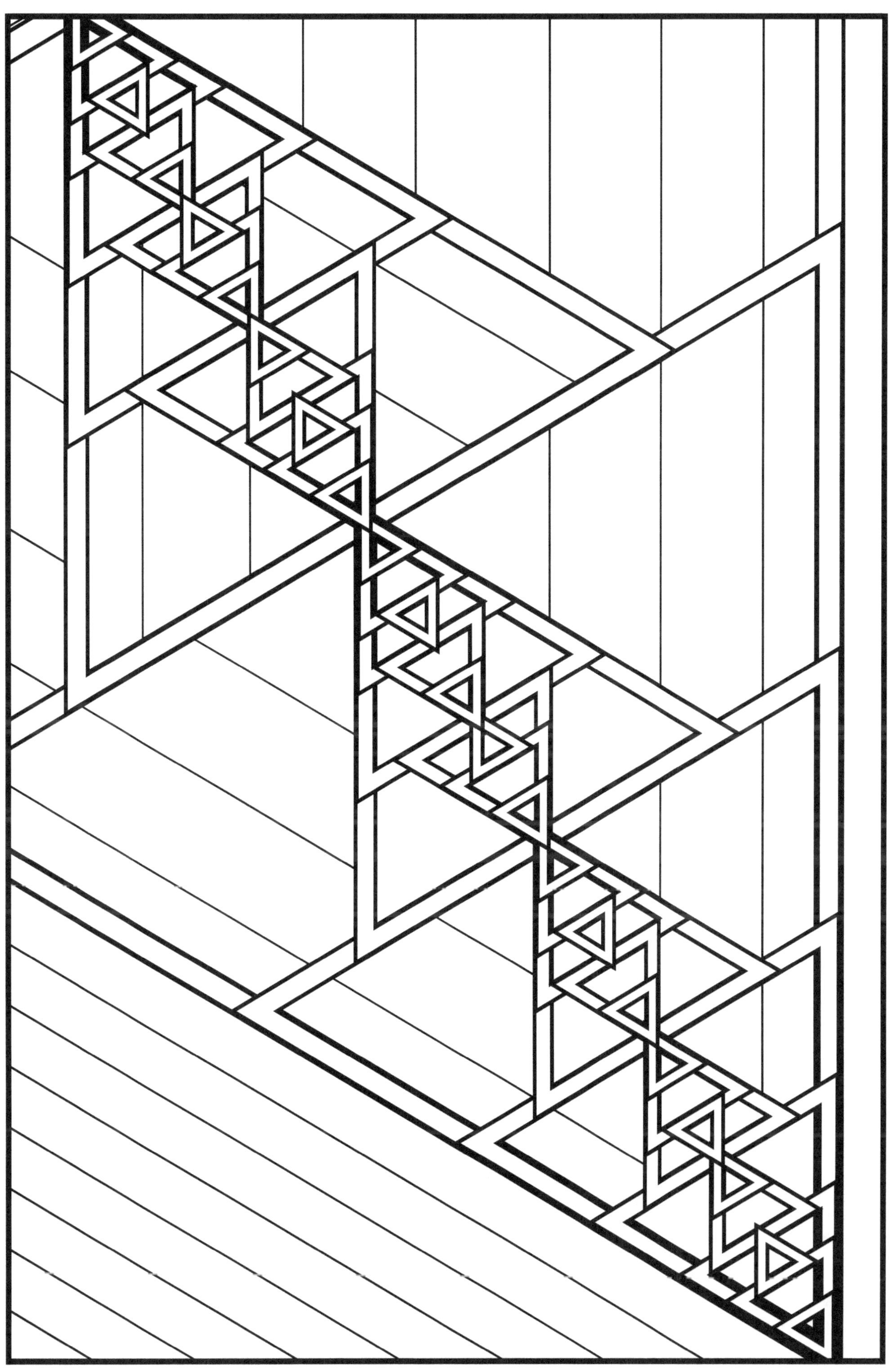

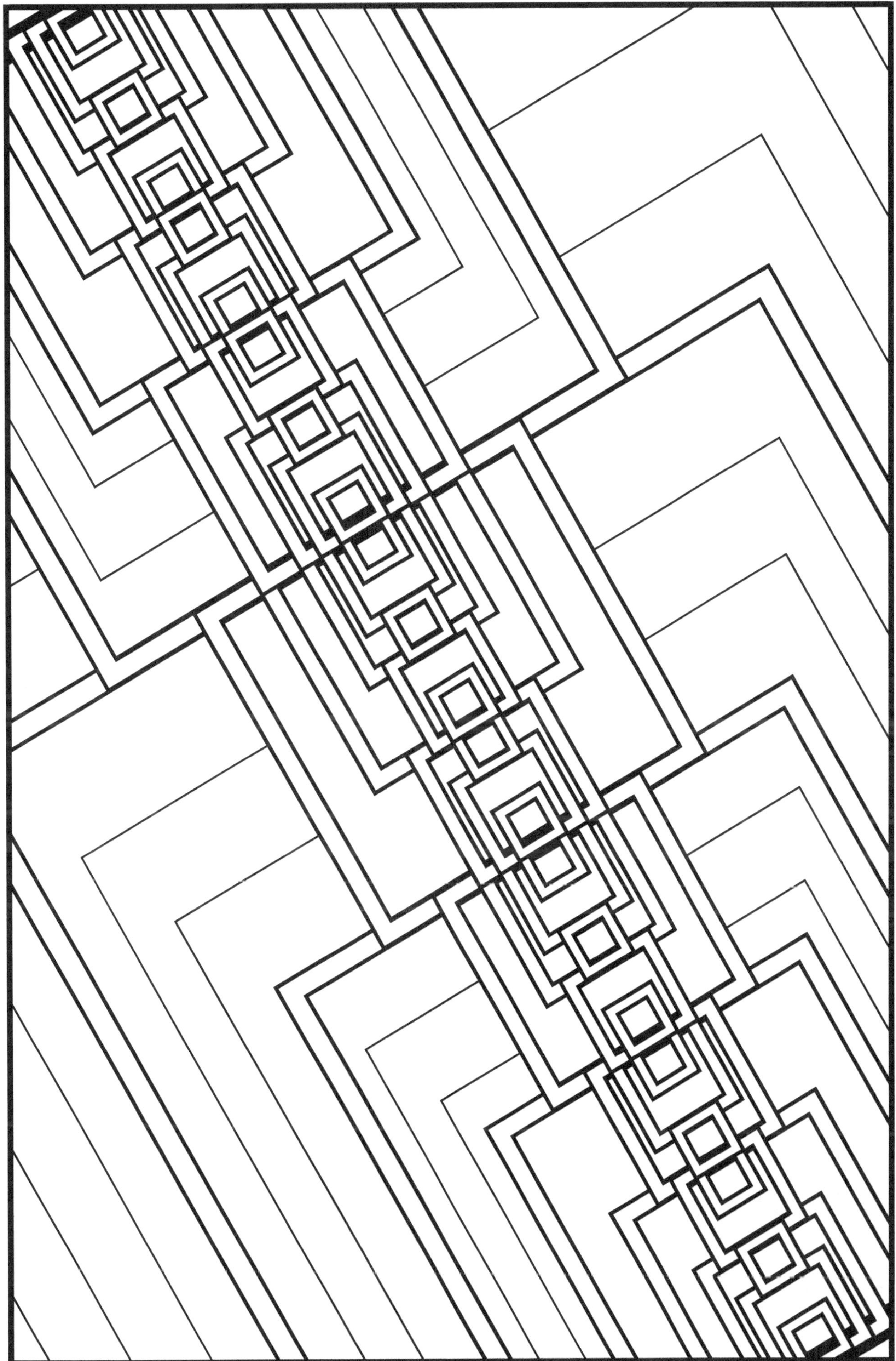

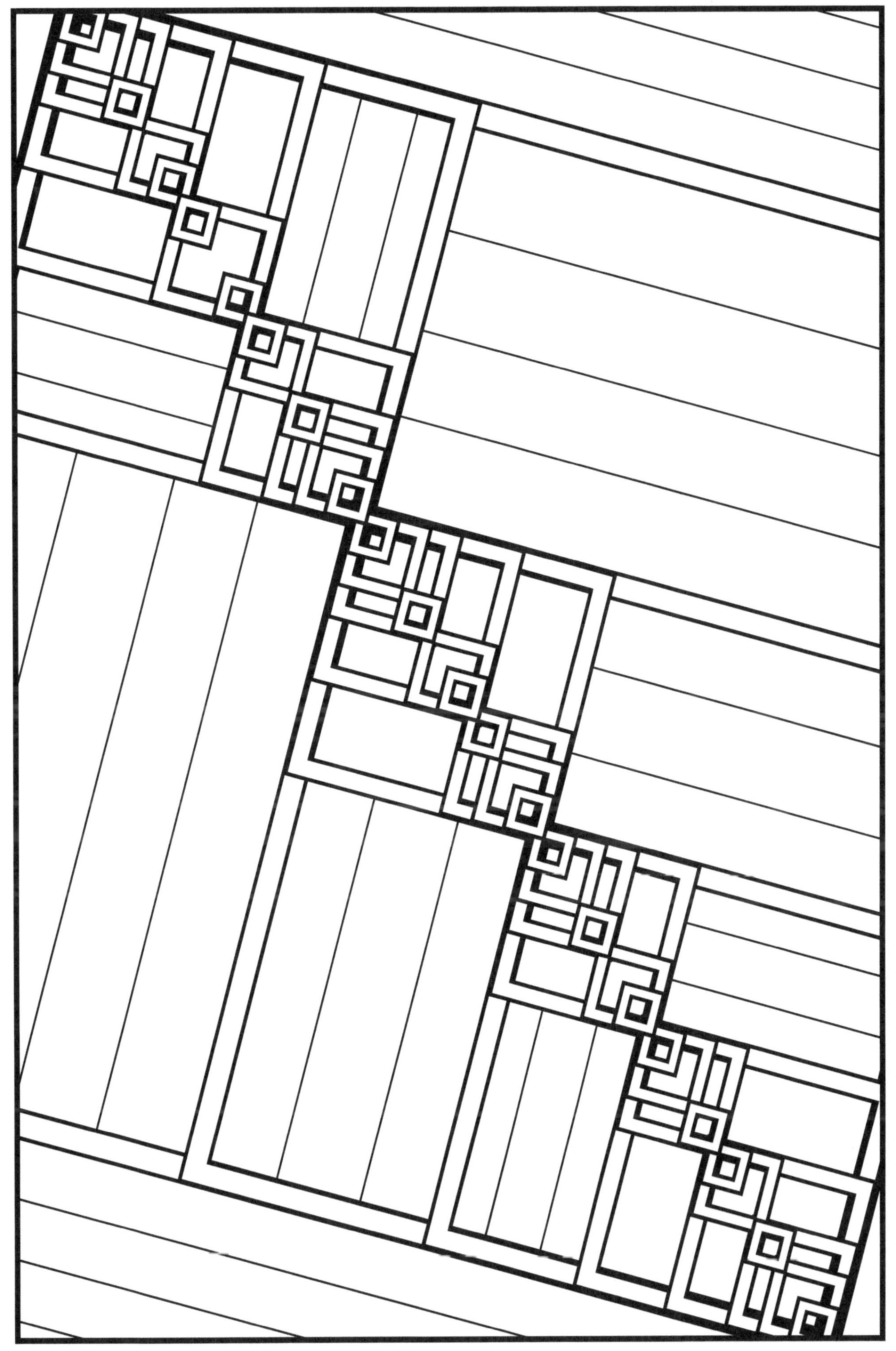

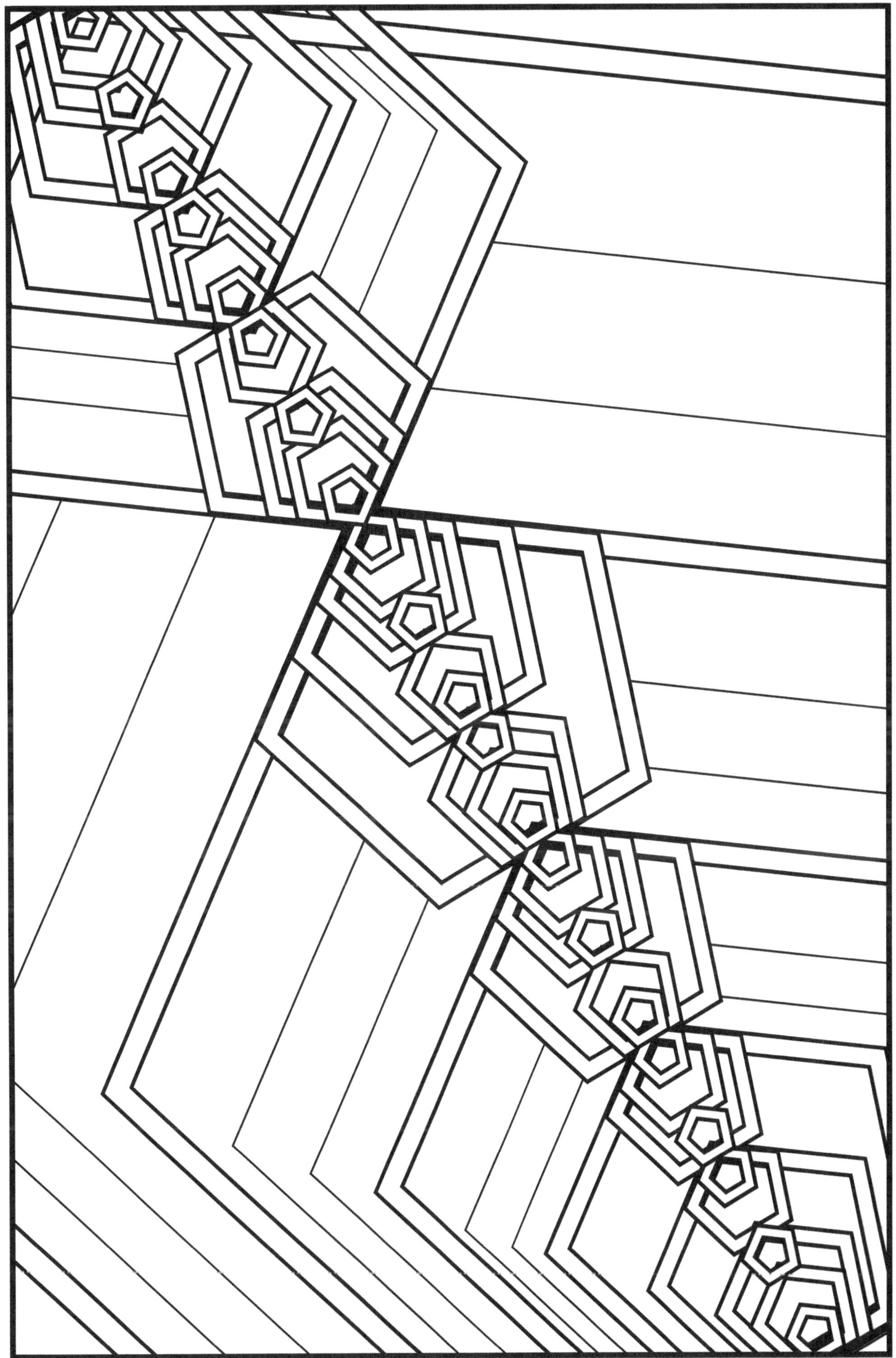

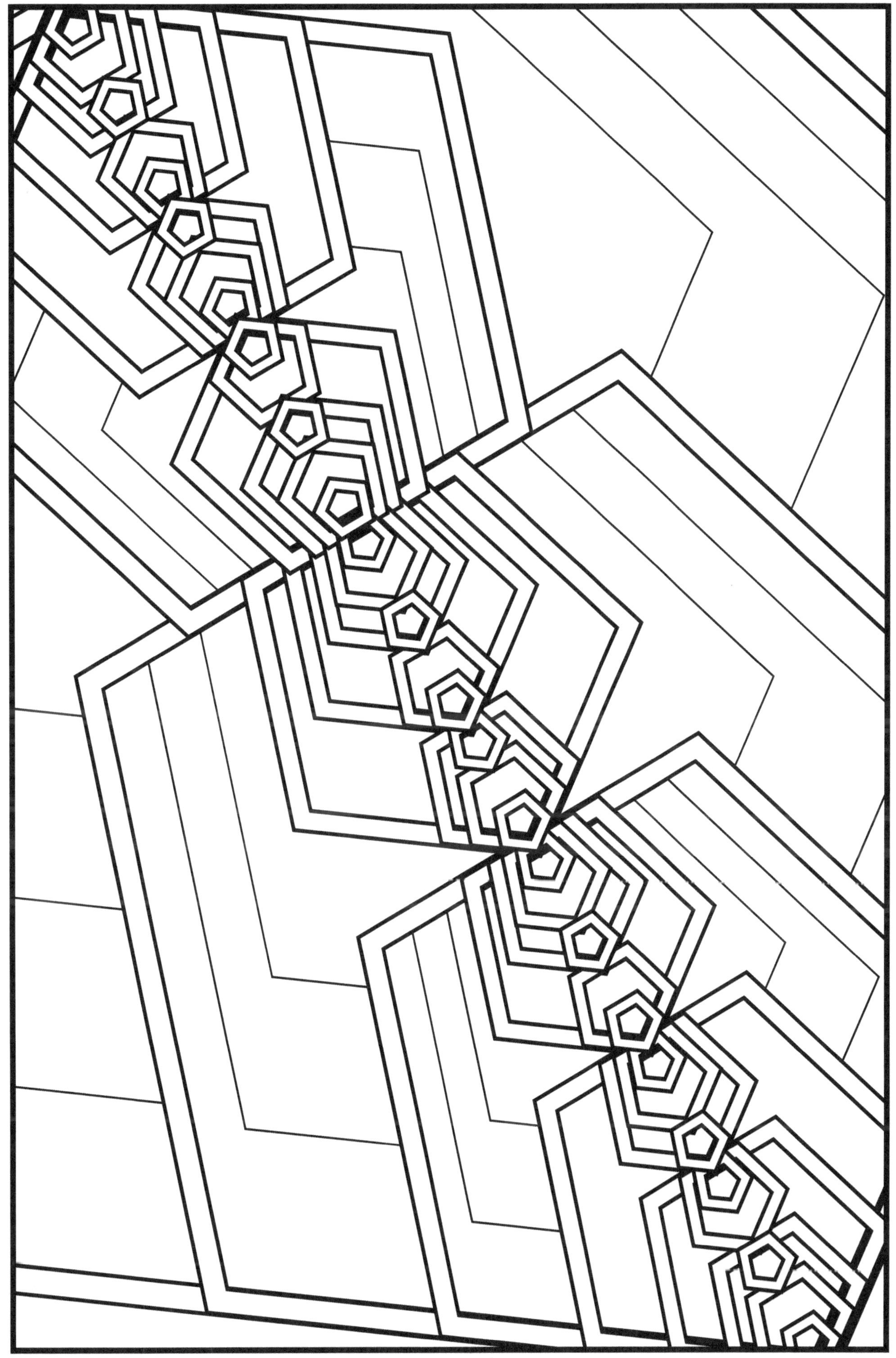

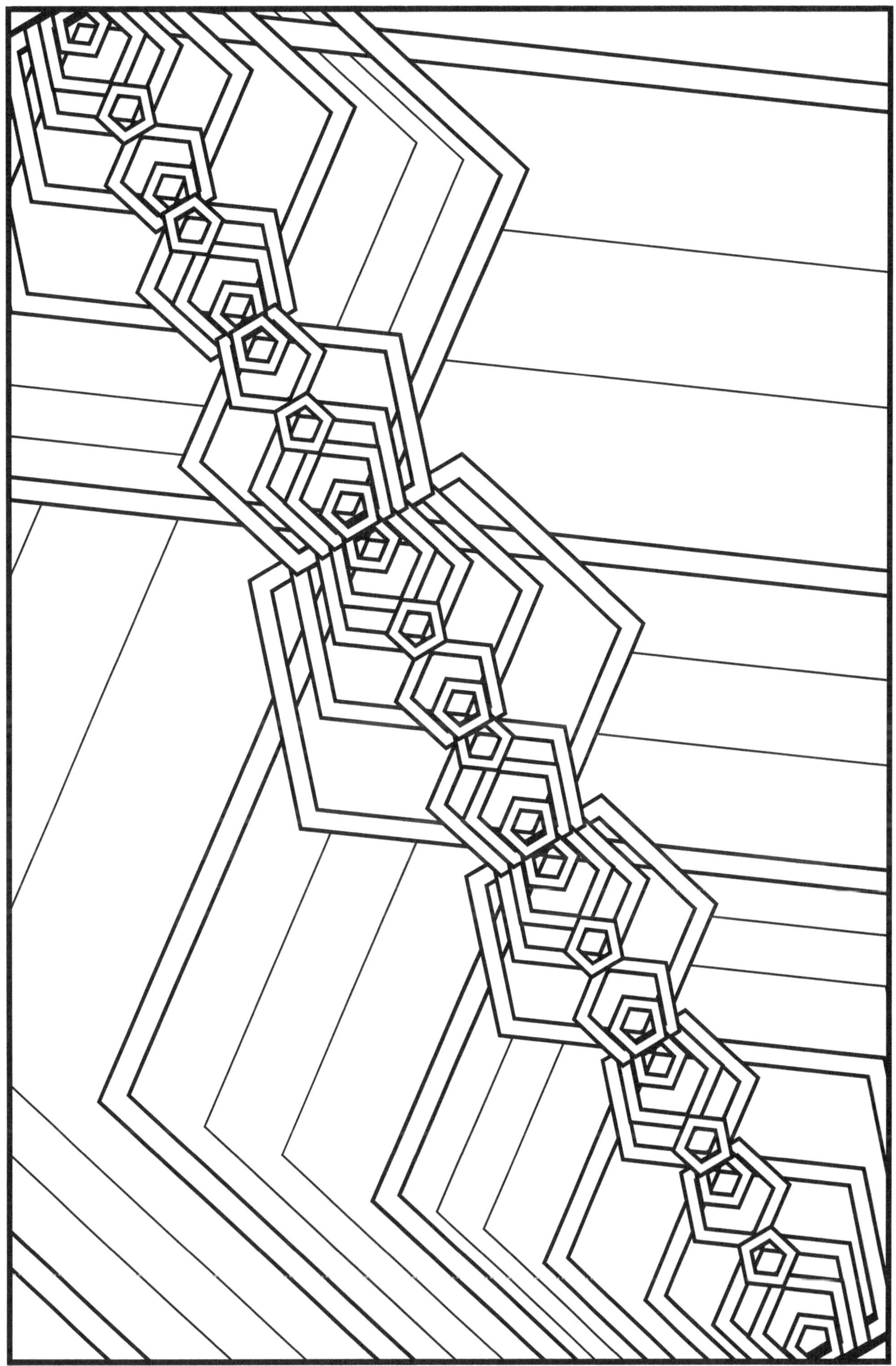

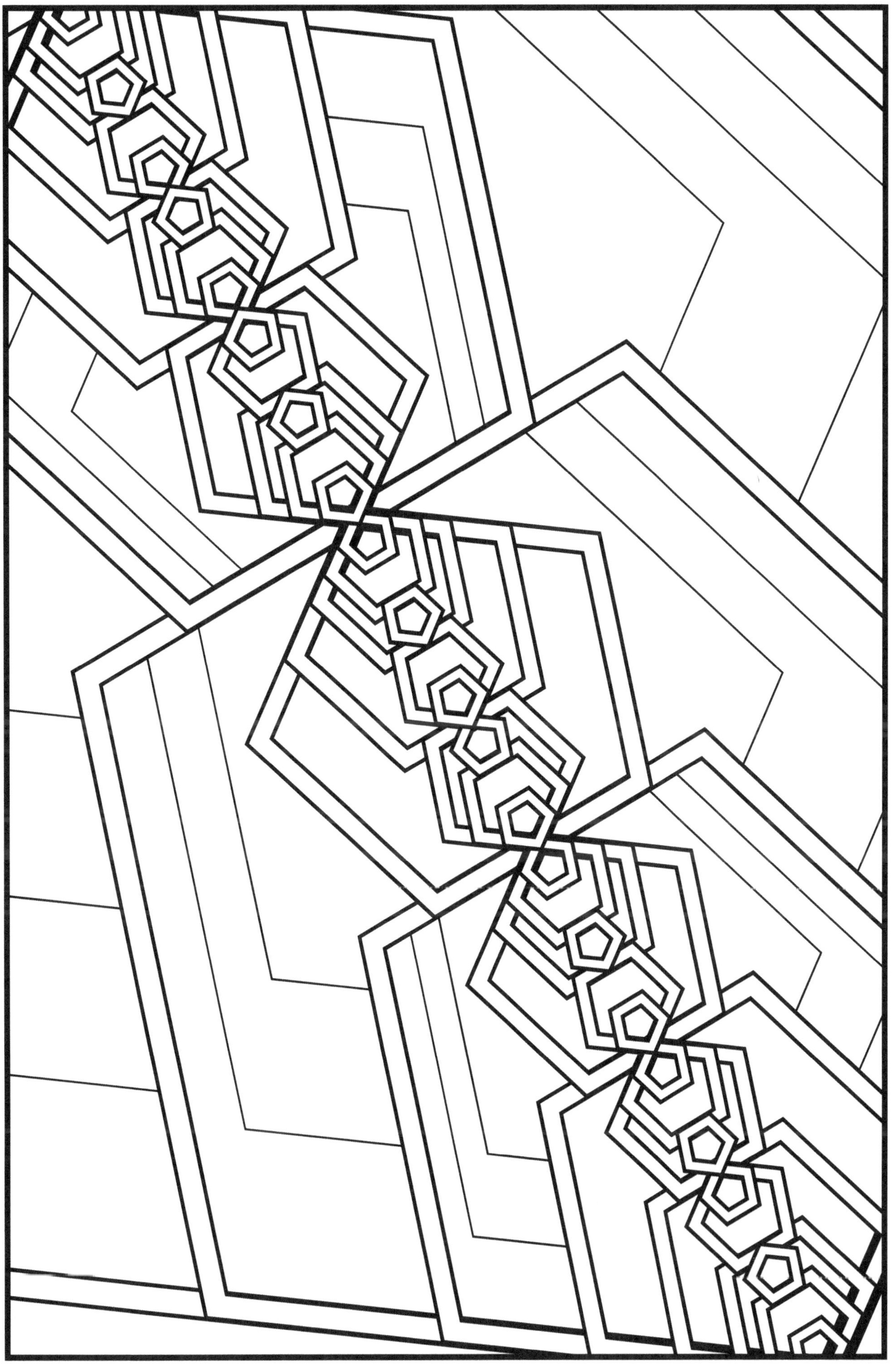

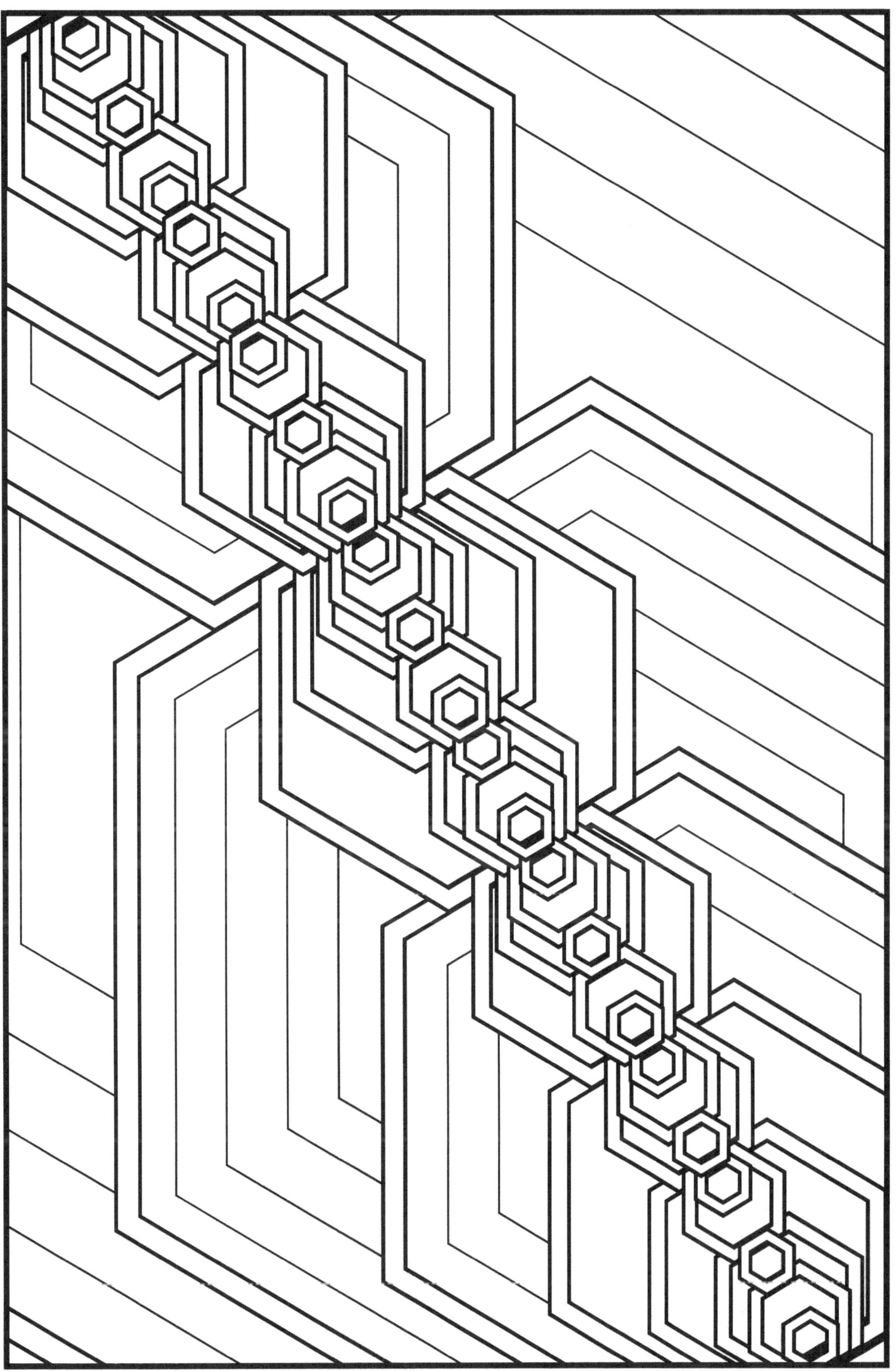

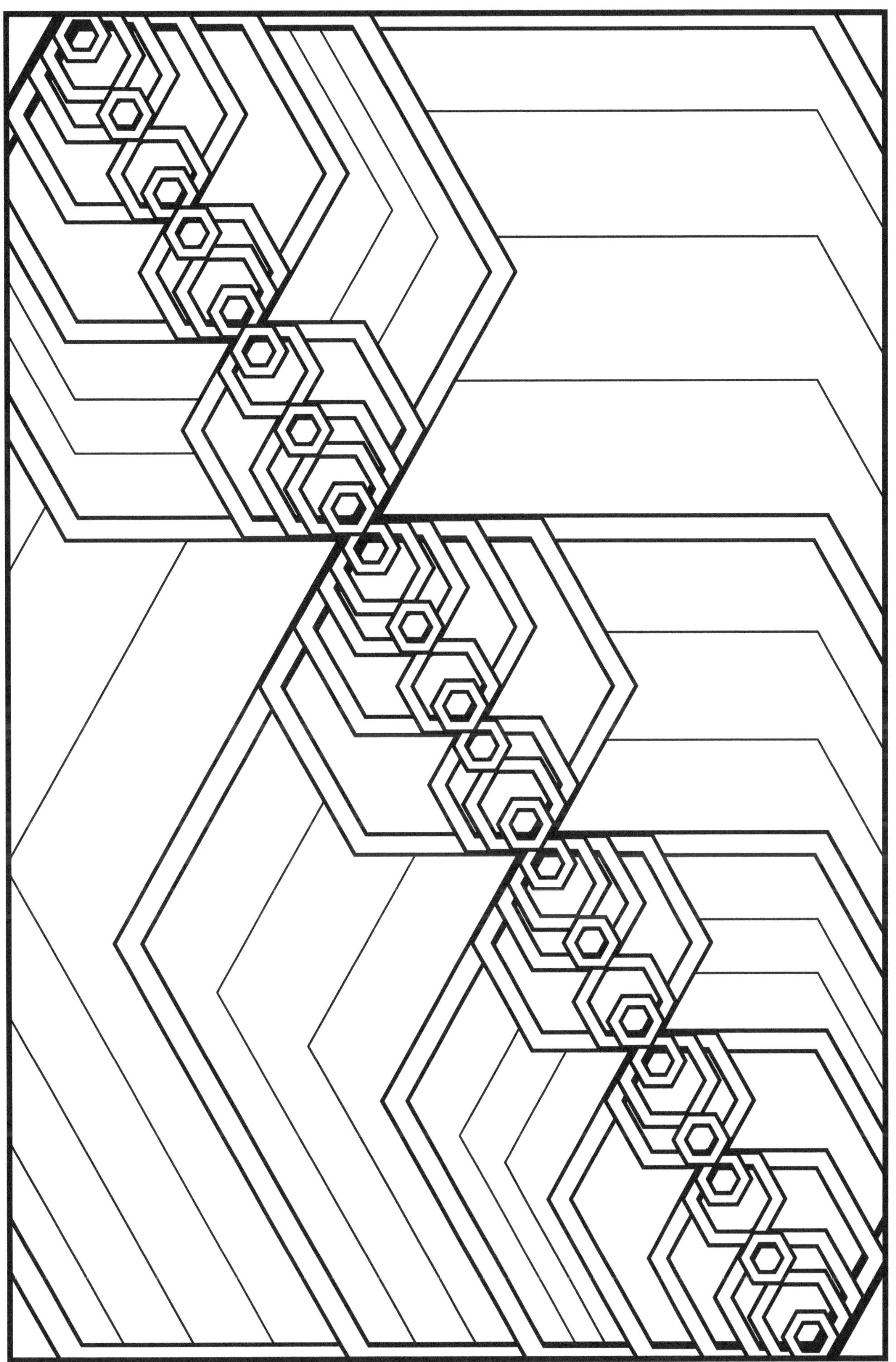

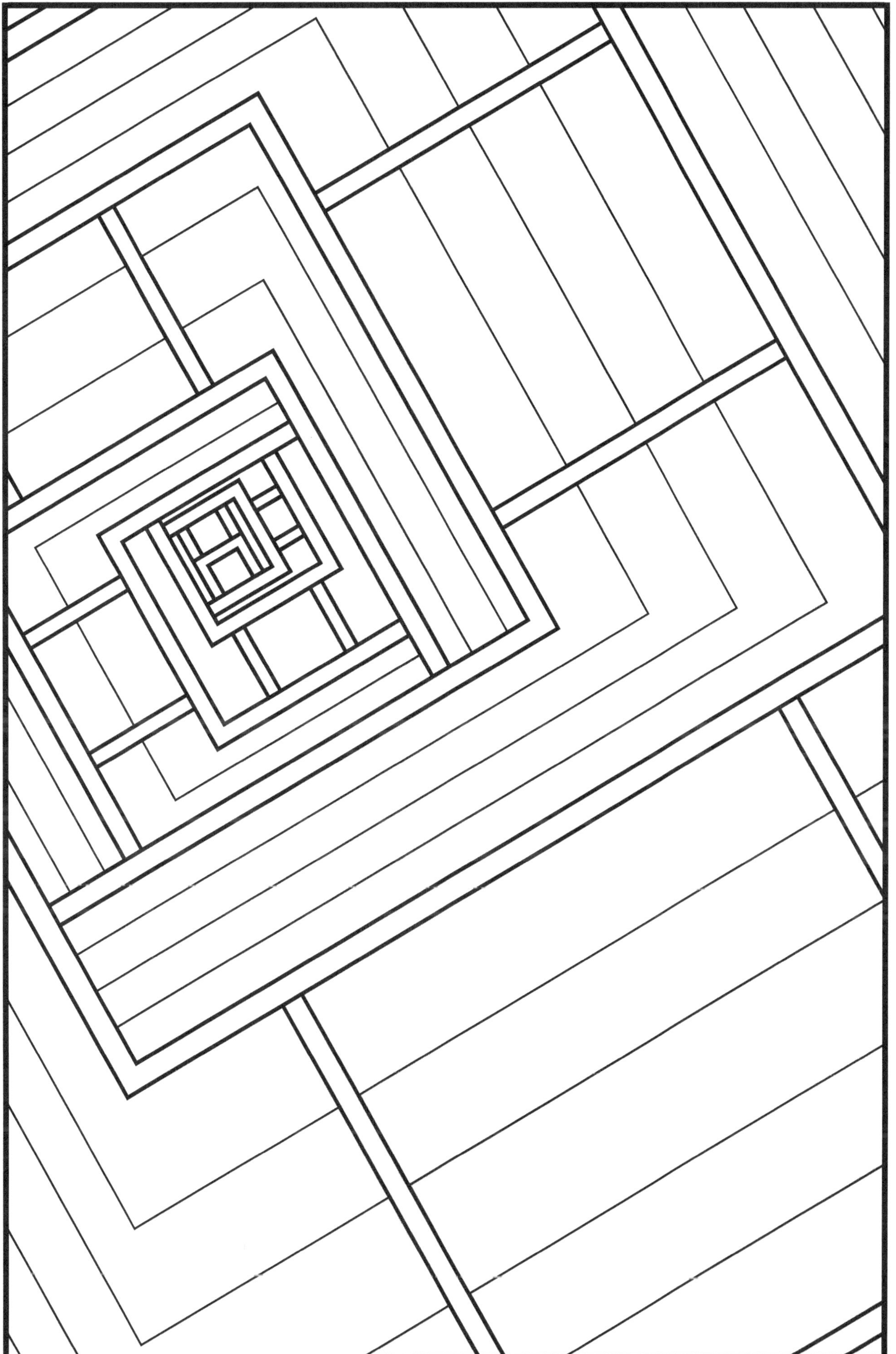

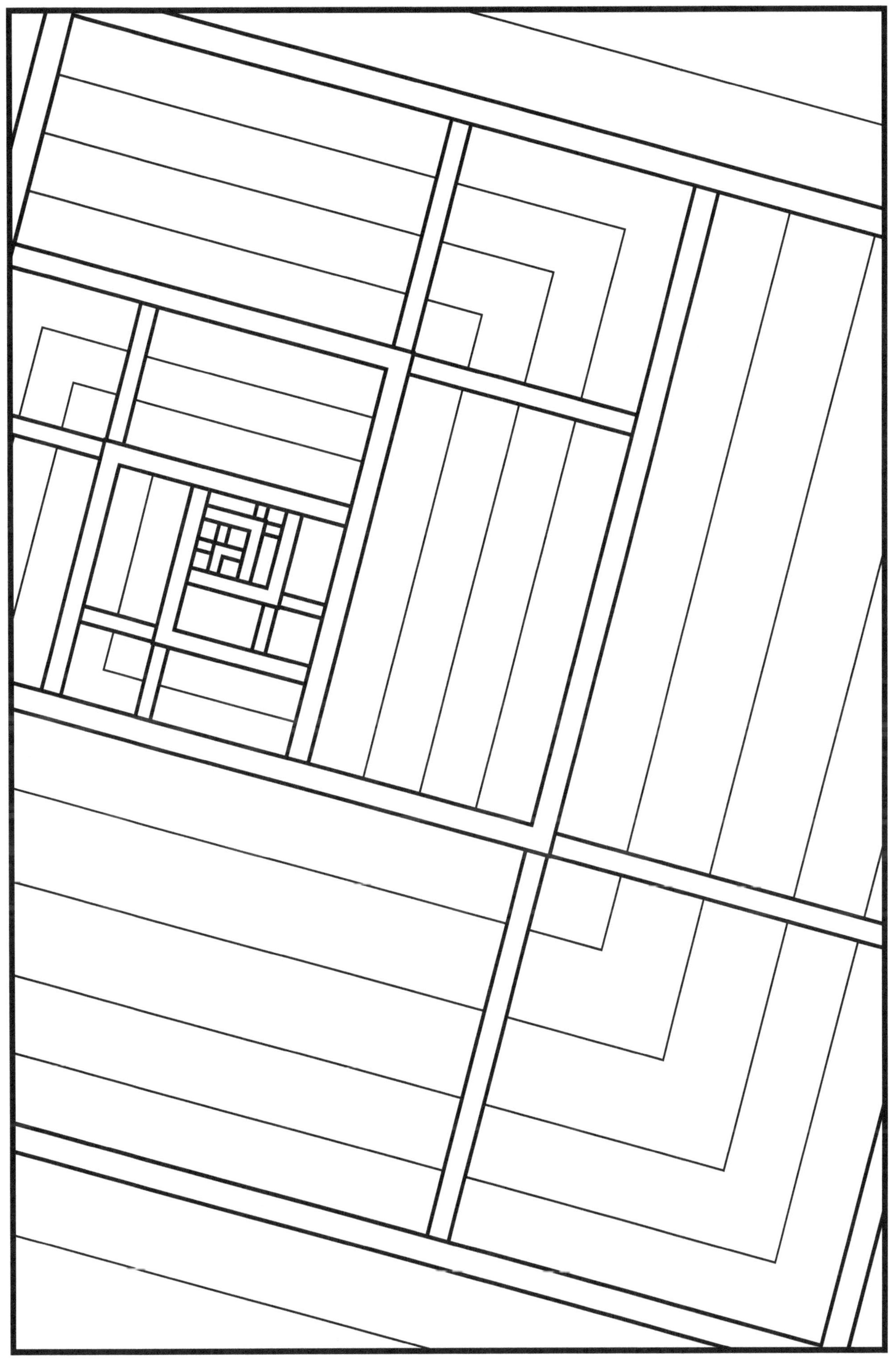

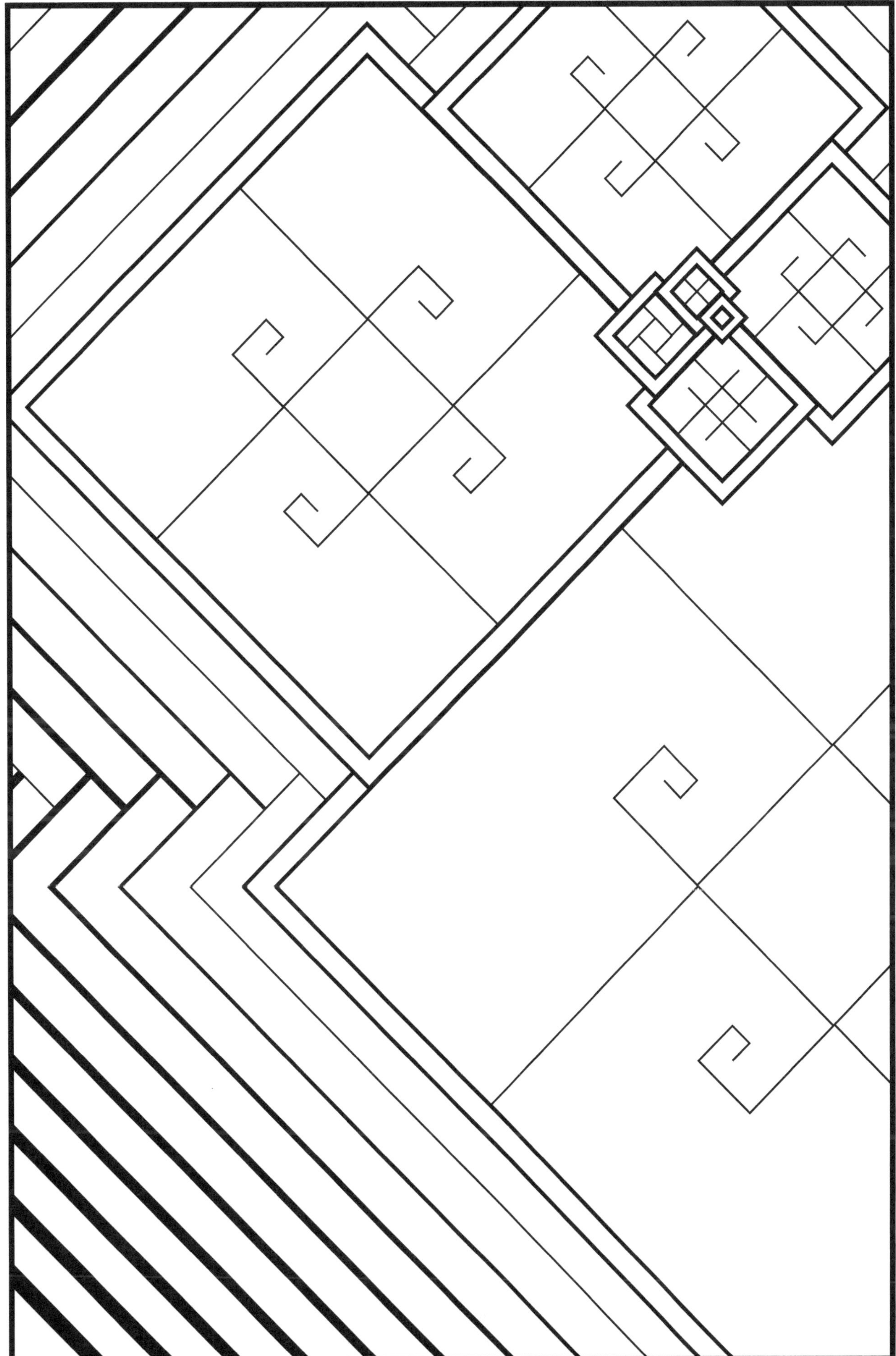

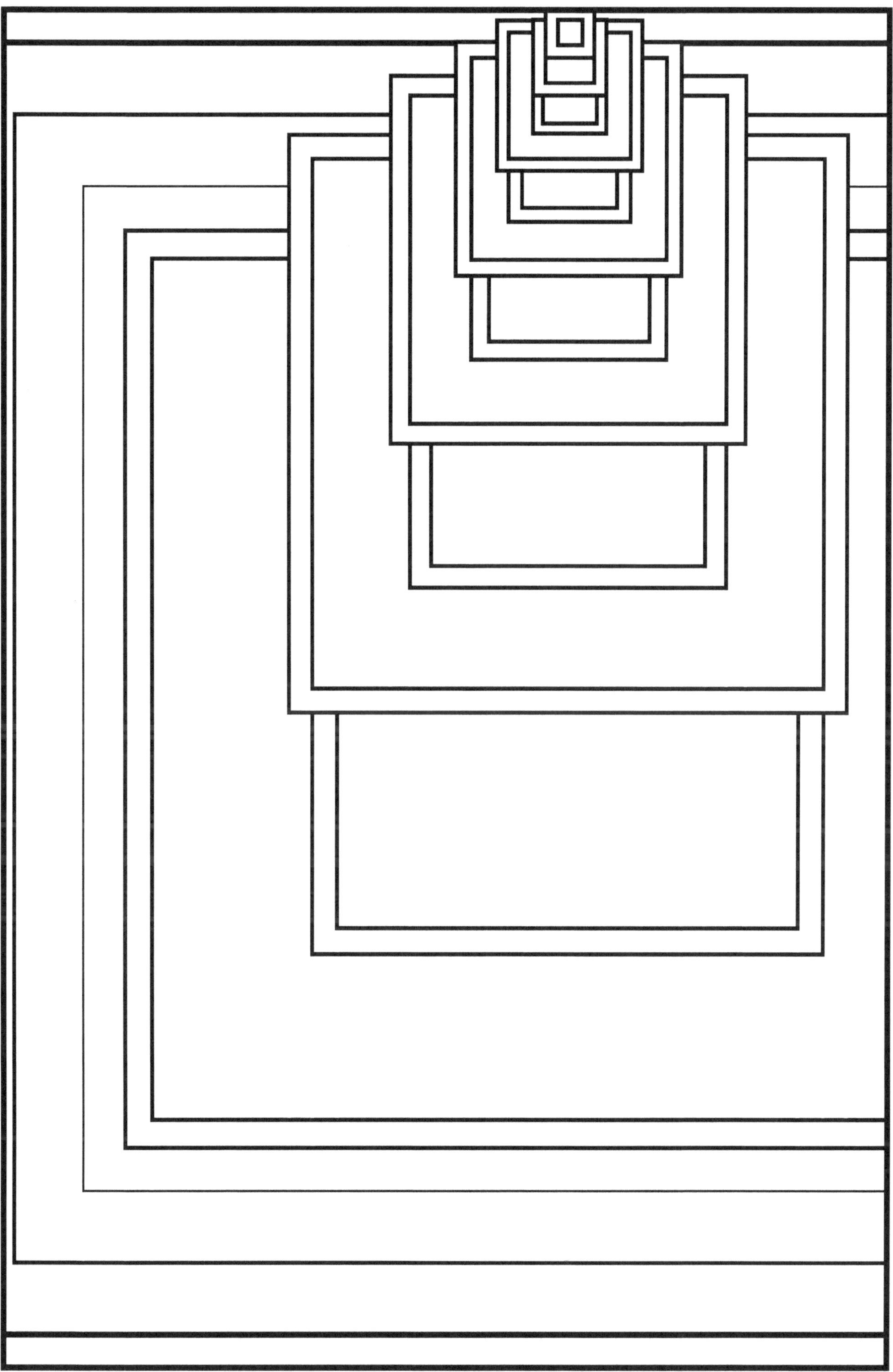

FIBONACCI·DESIGNS·2

SAMPLE·PAGE

GEOMETRIC·DESIGNS·1

SAMPLE·PAGE

IMPOSSIBLE·DESIGNS·1

SAMPLE·PAGE